THIS WALKER BOOK BELONGS TO:

_____

_____

_____

_____

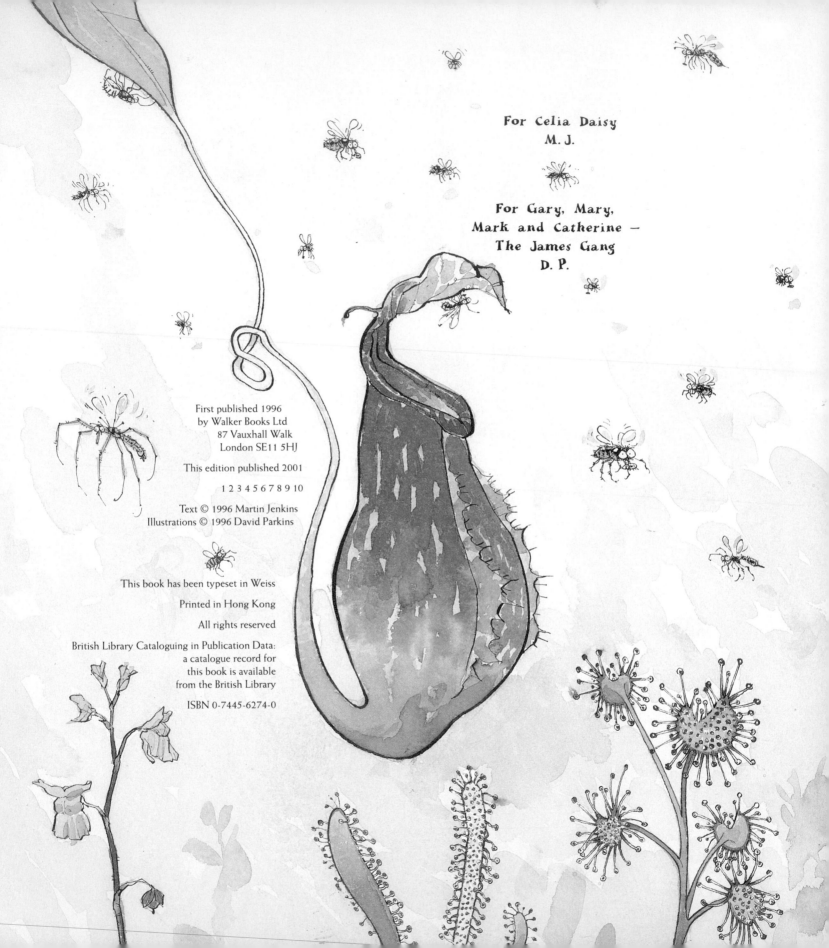

For Celia Daisy
M. J.

For Gary, Mary,
Mark and Catherine —
The James Gang
D. P.

First published 1996
by Walker Books Ltd
87 Vauxhall Walk
London SE11 5HJ

This edition published 2001

1 2 3 4 5 6 7 8 9 10

Text © 1996 Martin Jenkins
Illustrations © 1996 David Parkins

This book has been typeset in Weiss

Printed in Hong Kong

British Library Cataloguing in Publication Data:
a catalogue record for
this book is available
from the British Library

ISBN 0-7445-6274-0

Fly Traps!
Plants that bite back

Written by

Martin Jenkins

illustrated by

David Parkins

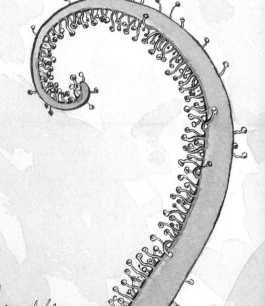

WALKER BOOKS
AND SUBSIDIARIES
LONDON · BOSTON · SYDNEY

People do all sorts of things in their spare time. There are yogurt-pot collectors and people who make models out of bottle tops. There are beetle-spotters and giant-leek growers.

Me, I like watching plants
that eat animals.

Plants that eat animals are called
carnivorous plants.

There are hundreds of different kinds
and they grow all around the world.

It all started with a plant I found in a pond. It had little yellow flowers sticking out of the water. Under the water there were tangled stems with hundreds of tiny bubbles on them. A friend told me it was called a bladderwort.

There are over
200 different kinds of
bladderwort. Most of them
grow in ponds and rivers.
They are usually quite
small, with narrow
leaves and stems.

She said the bubbles on the stems were the bladders. Each one had a trapdoor shut tight, with little trigger hairs around it.

To set its traps, a bladderwort sucks the water out of its bladders.

Whenever a water flea or other bug touched a hair, the trapdoor swung back and in the bug went.

When a trapdoor opens, water rushes in, dragging the bug in with it.

Then the trapdoor jammed shut and there was no way out. All in the twinkling of an eye.

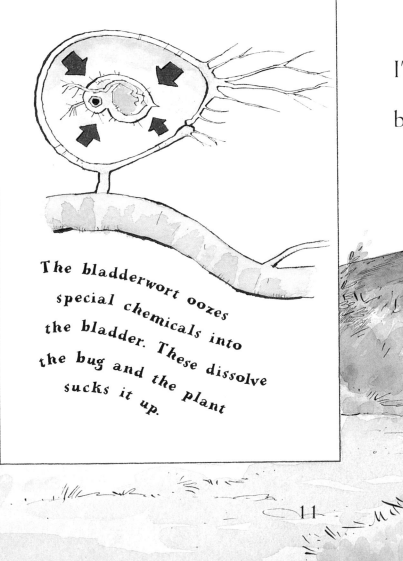

The bladderwort oozes special chemicals into the bladder. These dissolve the bug and the plant sucks it up.

Gosh, that's clever, I thought. The trouble was, the traps on my plant were so small and so quick that I couldn't really see them work.

Well, I decided, I'll just have to find a bigger carnivorous plant. So I did.

I had to climb a mountain, mark you, and walk

through all its boggiest, mossiest places.

But there in the moss were little red plants,

shining in the sun. I thought they were covered

in dewdrops, but they weren't. They were

sundews, and the shiny bits were sticky

like honey. I'm sure you can guess

what they were for.

When a bug gets stuck on a sundew, the leaf curls up slowly around it.

Then the soft bits of the bug are dissolved by chemicals and eaten.

I had to leave the sundews when the clouds rolled in. But as soon as I got home, I sent off for some sundew seeds of my own.

Afterwards, the leaf opens up again and the leftover bug bits fall off.

Butterworts are carnivorous plants, too, and often grow in the same places as sundews. They have flat leaves like flypaper. Little bugs stick to the leaves and slowly dissolve.

The seeds weren't just for ordinary sundews, though. They were for Giant African sundews. I sowed them in a pot of moss and covered it with glass.

I watered the pot every day, with rainwater straight from the water barrel. Soon the seeds started to sprout and I had dozens of baby sundews.

They grew and grew, until they were nearly big enough to start catching things.

Then one day I watered them with the wrong sort of water — and every single one died.

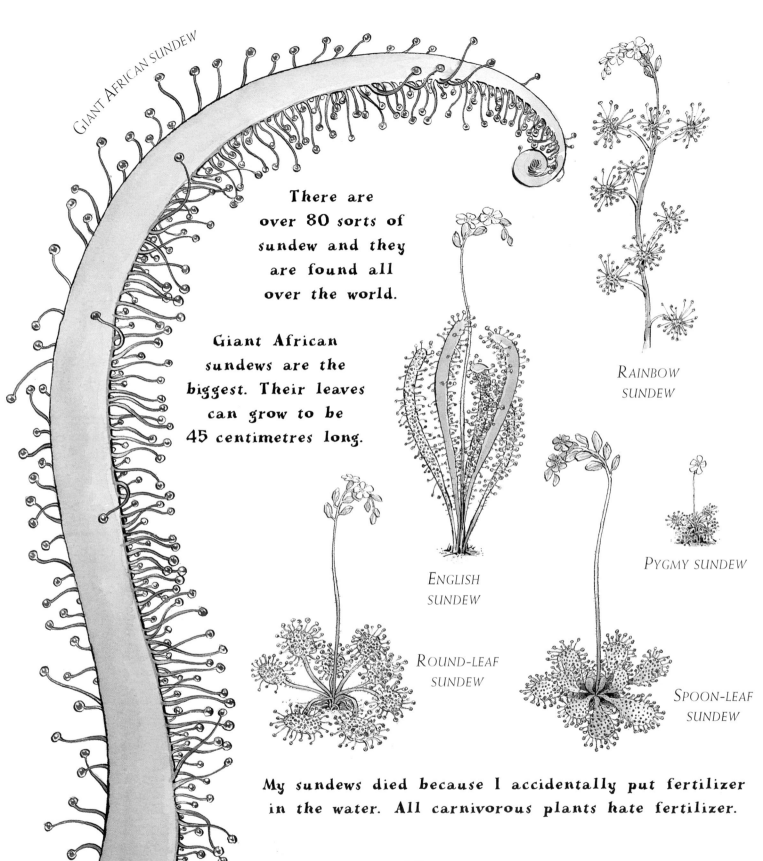

GIANT AFRICAN SUNDEW

There are over 80 sorts of sundew and they are found all over the world.

Giant African sundews are the biggest. Their leaves can grow to be 45 centimetres long.

RAINBOW SUNDEW

ENGLISH SUNDEW

PYGMY SUNDEW

ROUND-LEAF SUNDEW

SPOON-LEAF SUNDEW

My sundews died because I accidentally put fertilizer in the water. All carnivorous plants hate fertilizer.

15

I gave up on sundews after that,

but I did grow a Venus flytrap. It lived

on the windowsill and caught insects.

Each of its leaves had a hinge down

the middle, several little trigger hairs,

and a spiky rim.

When a fly or a wasp walked

over a leaf, it was perfectly safe

if it didn't touch any of the hairs.

It was even safe if it touched just

one of the hairs. But if it touched

two of the hairs, then...

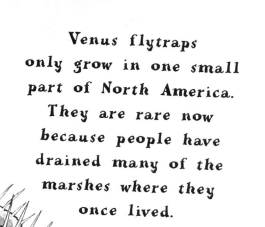

Venus flytraps
only grow in one small
part of North America.
They are rare now
because people have
drained many of the
marshes where they
once lived.

17

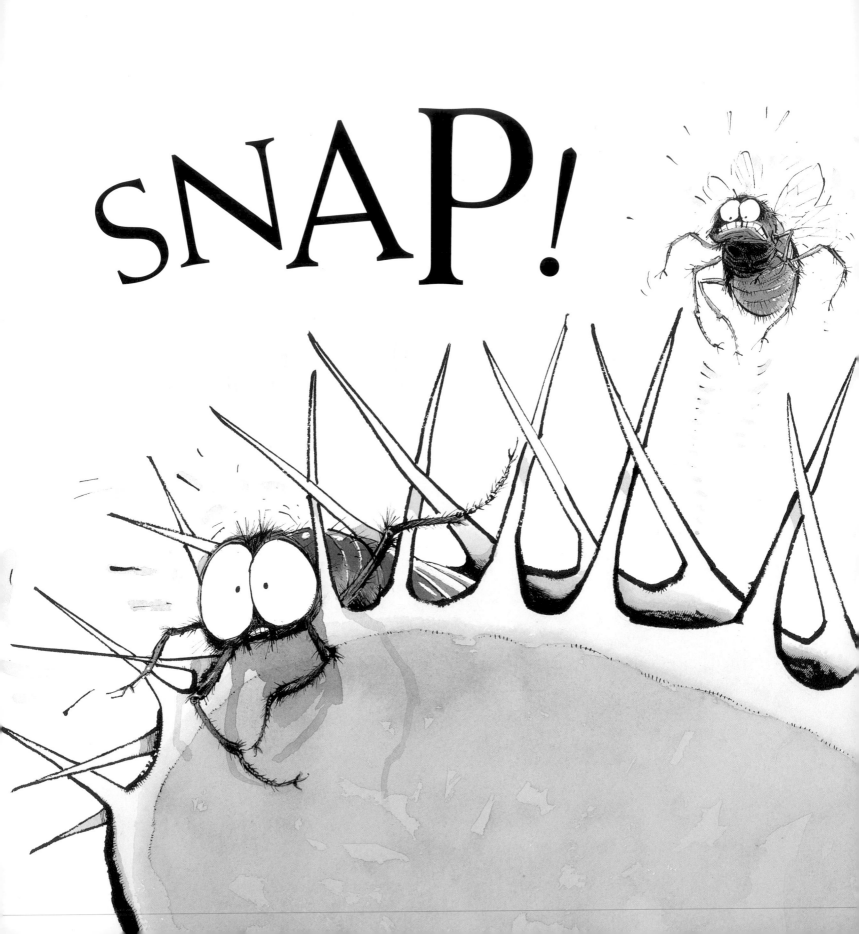

Small insects such as ants can escape from a Venus flytrap — they're not big enough to be worth eating.

But flies and wasps are a different story. Once caught, the more they struggle the tighter the leaf presses together.

When the leaf is fully closed, it begins to dissolve its victim.

19

My Venus flytrap seemed
quite happy, so I thought I'd try
growing something even bigger.
The next plant I got was a
cobra lily.

Cobra lilies get
their name because
their leaves look like
cobras, not because
they eat them!

This one caught insects, too, but it didn't actually do very much. It had leaves like funnels, with a slippery rim and a little pool at the bottom.

When insects crawled inside, they fell into the pool and couldn't climb out. So they stayed there and became bug soup for the lily.

Cobra lilies also come from North America. Their leaves can grow to be 45 centimetres high.

21

I was quite happy with my cobra lily. Surely it was the biggest carnivorous plant of all. But then my friend told me about pitcher plants.

Pitchers are even bigger, she said, but they are very difficult to grow. In that case, I thought, I'll just go and find some wild ones.

Pitcher plants are found in tropical countries. Like most other carnivorous plants, they usually grow where there is hardly any soil or where the soil is very poor.

So I went —

all the way to Malaysia.

And there, growing up the trees at the edge of the jungle, were hundreds of pitcher plants. Fat red ones, thin yellow ones, curly green ones, all waiting for flies.

The pitchers'
leaves look like
vases, and they
catch insects in
the same way that
cobra lilies do.

There are some sorts
of spider, and even some
small tree frogs, that
are able to live inside
the pitchers. They
cling to the slippery
sides and grab the
insects that fall in.

25

I didn't see the biggest

pitcher plant of all, though.

It's called the Rajah pitcher plant

and it grows on the tallest

mountain in Borneo.

It has pitchers the size of

footballs. People say it can even

catch some kinds of squirrel,

but I'm not convinced.

The mountain is called Kinabalu.
It is almost 4,000 metres high.
The Rajah pitcher plant only
grows there and it's even rarer
than the Venus flytrap.

One day I'll go and see for myself...

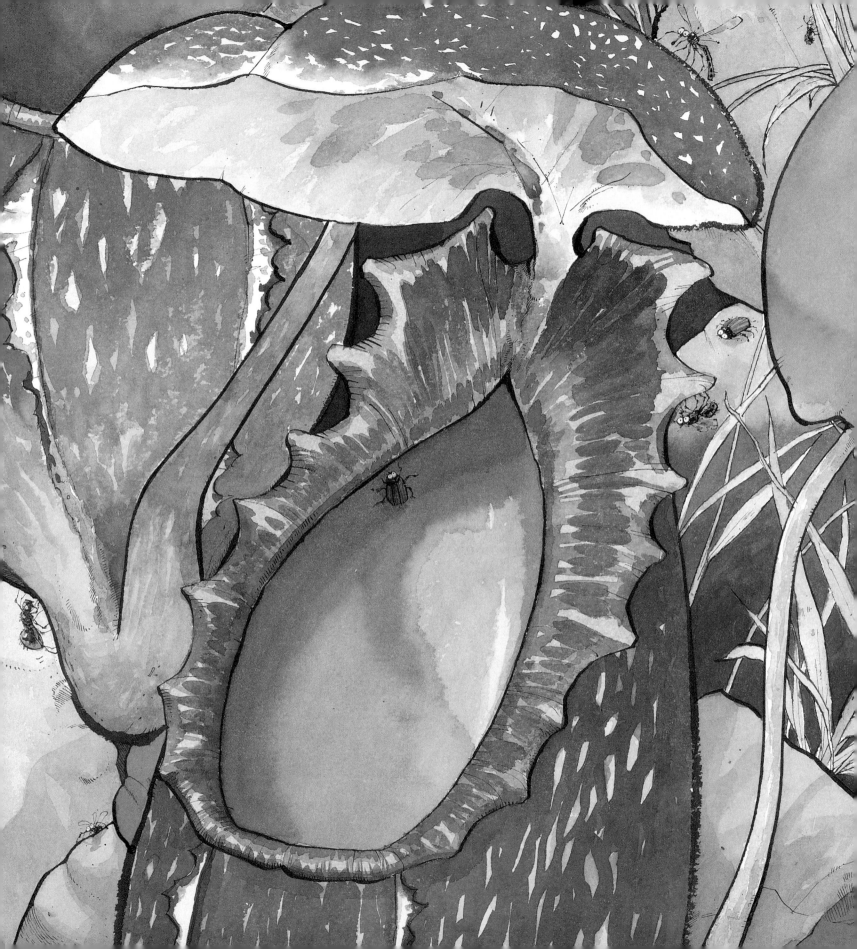

INDEX

Look up the pages to find out about all these carnivorous plant things. Don't forget to look at both kinds of words: this kind and **this kind**.

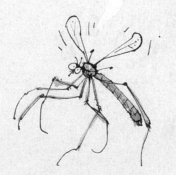

The author of this book,
MARTIN JENKINS, is a
conservationist biologist.
When not travelling to
faraway jungles and
mountain tops, he spends
most of his time writing
"serious things for the United
Nations and various governments".
He calls **Fly Traps! Plants that Bite Back**,
one of his first books for children,
"a plug for plants".

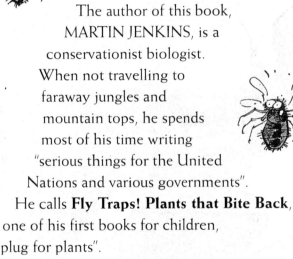

The illustrator of this book,
DAVID PARKINS, recalls, "When
I first started out as an illustrator,
I did a book on wildlife and spent
a year tramping around fields
drawing berries and birds.
So in a way, this book takes me
back to my roots, quite literally."

NOTES FOR TEACHERS

The READ AND WONDER series is an innovative and versatile resource for reading, thinking and discovery. Each book invites children to become excited about a topic, see how varied information books can be, and want to find out more.

Reading aloud The story form makes these books ideal for reading aloud – in their own right or as part of a cross-curricular topic, to a child or to a whole class. After you've introduced children to the books in this way, they can revisit and enjoy them again and again.

Shared reading Big Book editions are available for several titles, so children can read along, discuss the topic, and comment on the different ways information is presented – to wonder together.

Group and guided reading Children need to experience a range of reading materials. Information books like these help develop the skills of reading to learn, as part of learning to read. With the support of a reading group, children can become confident, flexible readers.

Paired reading It's fun to take turns to read the information in the main text or in the captions. With a partner, children can explore the pages to satisfy their curiosity and build their understanding.

Individual reading These books can be read for interest and pleasure by children at home and in school.

Research Once children have been introduced to these books through reading aloud, they can use them for independent or group research, as part of a curricular topic.

Children's own writing You can offer these books as strong models for children's own information writing. They can record their observations and findings about a topic, make field notes and sketches, and add extra snippets of information for the reader.

Above all, Read and Wonders are to be enjoyed, and encourage children to develop a lasting curiosity about the world they live in.

Sue Ellis, Centre for Language in Primary Education